Fantasy Faces

Grayscale Coloring Book for Adults

by

Ruth Sanderson

Colored by

_____

FANTASY FACES

Introduction

The twenty-four images in this book are close-up portraits from my original paintings, created over the course of my career as an illustrator and fantasy artist. I have carefully adjusted the pictures to create grayscale images suitable for coloring. Note: a few of these pictures are more detailed close-ups of images that appear in some of my other coloring books.

This book includes two full set of 24 images— in both lighter and darker versions, for you to try out and discover your preference. I prefer a darker grayscale that more closely reflects the tones from light to dark in the original paintings, though I always try to adjust both lighter and darker grayscale for an optimal coloring experience. Bright medium-value colors actually work great over darker grays, and you don't have to work as hard to build darks.

Turn to the back of the book for practice pages with six small portraits, along with suggested color combinations for six different skins tones and hair colors. There are also two pages of tips on applying and blending layers of colored pencils, on both the portraits and other parts of the pictures.

I would rate the level of difficulty in coloring these pictures at least an intermediate level, so having some knowledge and practice of coloring basics would be very helpful. If you consider yourself a beginner at grayscale coloring, or just would like to see how I approach coloring faces, I suggest you watch my Youtube video tutorials. I have one on coloring a light skintone and one on a darker skintone:

https://www.youtube.com/user/ruthsander

Join my RuthSandersonArt coloring group on Facebook
—and post your pictures!

Happy Coloring!
Ruth

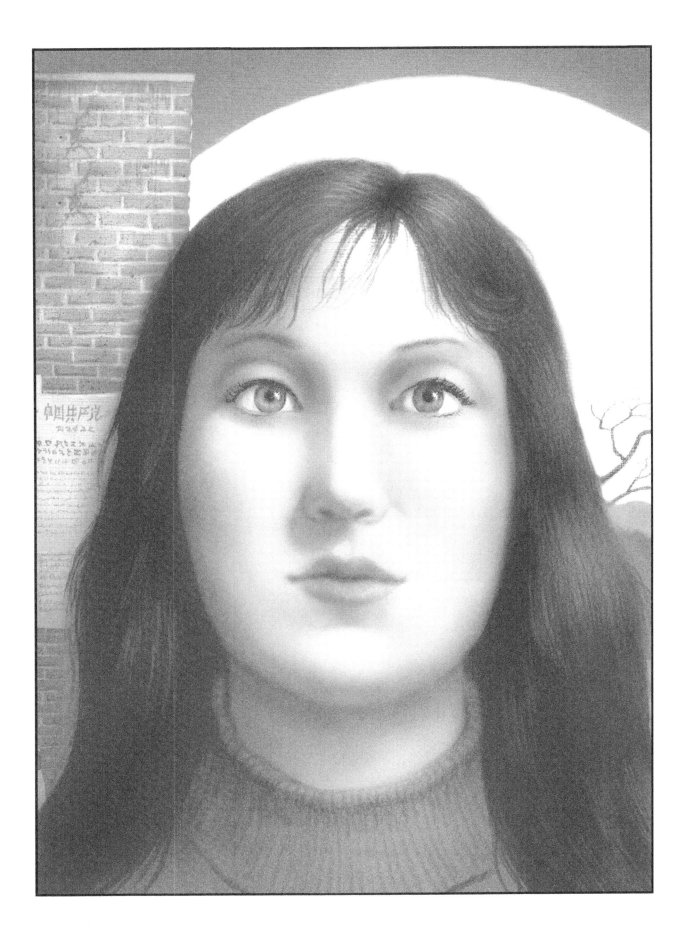

Note: The following pages contain a second set of images that are a little darker, for those who prefer coloring pictures that have a full tonal range similar to the original paintings. The practice pages at the back of the book use the darker grayscale images, as that is my personal preference in coloring over grayscale.

FANTASY FACES: Colored Pencil Tips

I prefer using colored pencils for grayscale coloring. The tonal shading shows through the colors to give the pictures depth and a realistic look. The pencils I like the best are Prismacolor Premiers, and for simplicity's sake the tutorials here are using only those pencils. Many people color with other brands, pan pastels and other media, and I encouage you to experiment and find your own preferred way of working. My way is not the "right way" or the only way!

The original pictures in this book were realistic oil paintings, rendered with a source of light on the subject. Try to keep a similar tonal pattern to the original picture, choosing pale colors for light areas, medium tones of the same color family for shadow areas, etc, as you plan your color palette. In this way your pictures will also look like there is light shining on the subjects.

 The key to coloring with colored pencils is to use light pressure, "gliding" your pencil across the image, and many "layers," going over the same area multiple times, until the gray is covered with "glazes" of even color.

You can color over someone's **entire** head of hair, for instance, with a rich medium tone of a color, always following the direction the hair is flowing with your strokes, pressing lightly in light areas, and adding extra layers of color in grayer areas. The grays underneath will still show through your layers of color and define the light and dark areas of the hair and all the subtle gradations will show. Add a lighter color to the highlight area, and a darker color to the deepest shadows. Overlap all areas again, back and forth **with all three colors** in their respective sections, until you are satisfied with the effect.

Of course you can use more than three colors for hair, and more than three colors for skin, but you can also keep your palette simpler if you prefer. Sometimes just one color over an area is enough, and the grays showing through underneath will define the details.

 For clothing, choose two versions of the same color, one lighter for the light areas, and one medium tone for the shadows. Color over **all the gray** with even, light-pressure layers. Accent the creases with a bit more pressure on the same medium-tone pencil, for vibrant shadows. I usually save dark colors, if needed, for last, sometimes adding accents and an occasional outline. After adding darks, I suggest you go over that same area again with a medium tone color for a smoother look. (Or burnish for an even smoother look--see the next page.)

I suggest the following steps when coloring faces, but find your own preferred methods. Note: The practice portraits are from the darker grayscale versions of the pictures, my preference for grayscale coloring. (And I do suggest finishing the background and hair first.)

1. Start with (usually 4) light pressure layers of each color. Add each color in the order listed, or start with darkest colors if you prefer. Use light colors over white and pale gray areas, medium and darker colors over darker grays. Add more layers of your most saturated color flesh tone (like Peach for light skin and Burnt Ochre for the darkest skin) in the transitions from light to shadow, as those areas in a realistic portrait would be brighter. Use darks if needed and add layers on top of the dark color afterward with a medium tone to smooth them. Use your own judgement for how much pigment to add to faces—some people prefer using fewer layers, letting more gray show through.

2. Try a combo of Peach and Nectar for natural-looking lips, or add Blush Pink and/or Pink over that base.Add reds over that base if you want a "lipstick" look. Make lower lip lighter.

3. Repeat the layering as needed. Keep a light hand. Be patient! Again: **Overlap areas of transition between a light area and a shadow area with"feathered" layers of a mid-tone color.**

4. Use 949-Dark Brown or 946--Dark Umber for eyes, accents.

5. Try 953-Burnt Ochre if needed in nostrils, between lips, ears, eyelid crease. Soften with Nectar if it looks too dark.Try 941- Light Umber for deepening shadows under chin, if needed.

6. Burnish and blend using your preferred method. Here are the three I use:

1. Use a light color in each given area, slowly pressing harder to blend the colors and flatten the paper "tooth." I often use a more neutral color, such as Peach Beige (Combo #4) to burnish. If the picture looks good without burnishing, leave it alone. Sometimes for really dark skin I don't find it necessary to burnish the shadows. (My preference for faces is to blend with the pencils.)

2. Gamsol mineral spirits or another brand, applied with a paper blending stump, a pointy make-up Q-tip, or a brush. I often use this method for clothing, hair, and backgrounds.

3. A colorless marker. Note: If you use Gamsol or a colorless marker, you can layer with more pencil. I do find **colorless pencil blenders** sometimes pick up the gray under the colors, so I avoid them.

Whew! Portraits are perhaps the most challenging subjects to color with colored pencils.

With practice you will keep improving, so don't get discouraged!

FANTASY FACES PRACTICE SHEET ---- Prismacolor Premiers

See the previous page for suggestions for lips, features, and accents. Photocopy these pages if you'd like to practice more times. Create your own color combinations, too. Try Deco Peach 1013* for brighter tones on light faces. There are so many ways to approach fleshtones, and no one "right way." Experiment!

SKIN Color Combo #1   HAIR

940---Cream
927----Light peach
997-----Beige   940---Sand
939---Peach   1033-Mineral Orange
928----Blush Pink   945---Sienna Brown
1092---Nectar*   946---Dark Brown
1019--- Rosy Beige

SKIN Color Combo #2

997-----Beige
939----Peach
928----Blush Pink   1012--Jasmine
1092---Nectar*   942--Yellow Ochre
1017---Clay Rose   1034--Goldenrod
1085---Peach Beige*   941--Light Umber
945---Sienna Brown

SKIN Color Combo #3

997-----Beige
1085---Peach Beige*
1019---Rosy Beige
939---Peach
1092---Nectar*   1019--Rosy Beige
1017 Clay Rose   1081--Chestnut
941---Light Umber   946---Dark Brown

* The skin colors marked with an asterick are not in the Prismacolor portrait set, but I find them very useful.

FANTASY FACES PRACTICE SHEET--- **Prismacolor Premiers**

SKIN Color Combo #4
997---Beige
1085---Peach Beige
939---Peach
1092---Nectar
929----Pink (cheeks, lips)
1017---Clay Rose
943----Burnt Ochre
941---- Light Umber

HAIR
1059--10% Gray
1025--Periwinkle
901---Indigo
1082 Chocolate

SKIN Color Combo #5
1012--- Jasmine
1018--- Pink Rose
1092---Nectar
1033---Mineral Orange
1017---Clay Rose
929----Pink (cheeks, lips)
943----Burnt Ochre
941---- Light Umber

SKIN Color Combo #6
1085---Peach Beige
939---Peach
1092---Nectar
1019---Rosy Beige
1017---Clay Rose
1033---Mineral Orange
929----Pink (cheeks, lips)
943----Burnt Ochre
1082 Chocolate

HAIR
1019 Rosy Beige
945---Sienna Brown
946---Dark Brown

If you try out your own color combinations,
use the blank pages at the back of the book to note them and remember your favorites.

ABOUT THE ARTIST

A battered copy of Grimm's Fairy Tales was Ruth Sanderson's favorite reading as a child. Ruth is well known for her award-winning fantasy illustration and her fairy tales for children. New full-color picture book editions of her fairy tales, including retellings of *Cinderella, The Twelve Dancing Princesses, Papa Gatto,* and *The Snow Princess*, can be ordered from any local bookstore, Amazon, or from Interlink Publishing: www.interlinkbooks.com. Signed copies of her first edition out-of-print books are available through her website, ruthsanderson.com

Ruth has many other coloring books for adults currently available on Amazon, and more planned. Sign up for her quarterly newsletter at www.ruthsanderson.com and receive news on her latest releases, and a free coloring page download with each issue. For people who prefer to print on their paper of choice, downloadable PDFs of her books are available for purchase on Ruth's ETSY shop: www.etsy.com/shop/RuthSandersonArt.

ISBN: 9798644031382

Imprint: Independently Published

GOLDEN WOOD STUDIO
PO Box 285
Easthampton, MA 01027

Printed in the USA

Printed in Great Britain
by Amazon